Grade
3

Problem Solving

Written by Kathy Furgang

Illustrations by Ethan Long

FlashKids
An imprint of Sterling Children's Books

This book belongs to

_____

FLASH KIDS, STERLING, and the distinctive Sterling logo are registered trademarks of
Sterling Publishing Co., Inc.

Published by Sterling Publishing Co., Inc.
387 Park Avenue South, New York, NY 10016
Text and illustrations © 2006 by Flash Kids
Distributed in Canada by Sterling Publishing
c/o Canadian Manda Group, 165 Dufferin Street
Toronto, Ontario, Canada M6K 3H6
Distributed in the United Kingdom by GMC Distribution Services
Castle Place, 166 High Street, Lewes, East Sussex, England BN7 1XU
Distributed in Australia by Capricorn Link (Australia) Pty. Ltd.
P.O. Box 704, Windsor, NSW 2756, Australia

Sterling ISBN 978-1-4114-3469-1

Manufactured in China

Lot #:
4 6 8 10 9 7 5
03/12

For information about custom editions, special sales, premium and
corporate purchases, please contact Sterling Special Sales
Department at 800-805-5489 or specialsales@sterlingpublishing.com.

Cover design and production by Mada Design, Inc.

Dear Parent,

Learning to solve problems is one of the most important skills in math. *Problem Solving* will help your child to look at problems with a critical eye. The book includes fun activities that help your child to use logic, estimate, and choose a method to solve a problem. To get the most from *Problem Solving*, follow these simple steps:

- Find a comfortable place where you and your child can work quietly together.
- Encourage your child to go at his or her own pace.
- Offer your child help working out the problems if he or she needs it.
- Offer lots of praise and support.
- Let your child reward his or her work with the included stickers.
- Most of all, remember that learning should be fun! Take time to look at the pictures, laugh at the funny characters, and enjoy this special time spent together.

Welcome to the Big City!

Solving problems is important in the big city. To solve a problem, look at the facts you are given. Think about the questions you are asked. Fill in the blanks.

There are 6 people waiting at the taxi stand.

Of these people, 2 are women. How many are men?

1. _____ people are waiting for a taxi.

2. _____ women are waiting for a taxi.

3. _____ men are waiting for a taxi.

Good Morning!

Circle the operation that solves the problem.

1. The newspaper cost 50¢. Ron pays with a $5.00 bill.

   How much change should he get back? _____

        a) $5.00 – 50¢   b) $5.00 + 50¢

2. The newspaper has three sections. The news section is 16 pages

   long. The arts section is 22 pages long. The sports section is 20

   pages long. How many pages are in the paper? _____

        a) Add 3 + 16   b) Add 16 + 22 + 20

Look Up!

Use the chart to answer the questions.

Building A	90 stories tall
Building B	64 stories tall
Building C	76 stories tall
Building D	39 stories tall

1. How many stories does the shortest building have? _____

2. How many more stories does Building C have than Building B? _____

3. How many stories do all of the buildings together have? _____

Around Town

Cross out the sentence that is not needed to solve the problem.
Then solve the problem.

The school is 3 blocks from the museum.

The subway stops at the museum, but not the school.

How many blocks is it from the museum to the school? _____

Subway Stops

The subway stops every ten blocks. Fill in the missing information on the chart.
Then solve the problems.

SUBWAY STOPS
8th Street
18th Street
_____
38th Street
48th Street
_____
68th Street
_____
88th Street
98th Street
108th Street

1. How many stops is it from
   38th Street to 98th Street? _____

2. How many blocks is it from
   68th Street to 18th Street? _____

At the Theater

Read each problem to see if there is enough information to solve it.

Mark **enough information** or **not enough information**.

Solve the problems that have enough information.

1. The play starts in 10 minutes, but 3 people have not shown up yet.

   How many people will be late for the show? _____

   enough information   **not enough information**

2. The theater has 14 seats in the last row. It has 20 seats in the front

   row. How many more seats are in the front row than in the last? _____

   enough information   **not enough information**

3. Shows start at 3:30 PM and 8:00 PM. There is a 20-minute break

   in the middle of the show. How long is the play? _____

   enough information   **not enough information**

Farmer's Market

Use the sign to solve each problem.

flowers: $4.00
bananas: 50¢
apples: 50¢
pies: $4.00

1. Sara bought 2 apples, 2 bananas, and 1 cherry pie.
   How much did she spend in all? _____

2. How much do 2 bundles of flowers cost? _____

3. How much is an apple pie and a blueberry pie? _____

Strolling Through the Park

Read each problem to see if there is enough information to solve it.

Mark **enough information** or **not enough information**.

Solve the problems that have enough information.

1. Henry walks 4 miles an hour. Jack walks 2 miles an hour faster

   than Henry. How many miles an hour does Jack walk? _____

   enough information   **not enough information**

2. Sarah walks faster than Jennifer. Who will get to the park first? _____

   enough information   **not enough information**

3. Rita walked around the park 2 times. The path around the park

   is 3 miles long. How far did Rita walk? _____

   enough information   **not enough information**

Space Museum

Use the sign to solve each problem.

Planets	Comets	Asteroids	Black Holes	Stars
2:00	2:30	3:00	3:00	4:00

Margo wants to see as many shows as she can at the museum. Each show is 45 minutes long.

1. How many complete shows can Margo see? _____

2. Can Margo see shows about both asteroids and black holes?

   Why or why not? _____

3. Can Margo see shows about both planets and comets?

   Why or why not? _____

The World's Greatest Toy Store!

Circle the operation that will solve the problem, then solve each problem.

1. The store has a display of 25 toy vehicles. There are 8 cars, 4 buses, 7 dump trucks, and 6 tractors in the display. How many more dump trucks are there than tractors? _____

   a) 7 − 6   b) 8 − 6   c) 7 + 6   d) 8 + 6

2. There are 38 different board games for sale. Mark bought 3 games. How many different games can Tina now choose from? _____

   a) 3 + 38   b) 38 − 2   c) 38 − 3   d) 2 + 38

Take Me Out to the Ball Game

Cross out the sentences that are not needed to solve the problems.
Then solve the problems.

1. Hot pretzels cost 50¢. Drinks are $1.00. Nachos are $1.50.
   How much is a pretzel and a drink? _____

2. The home team scored 3 runs. The away team scored
   1 less run than the home team. It is the fifth inning.
   How many runs were scored in the game? _____

A Trip to the Museum

Solve the problems.

The city museum has 89 paintings, 56 sculptures, and 69 photographs.

1. How many more paintings do they have than photographs? _____

2. How many photographs and sculptures do they have? _____

3. How many pieces of art does the museum have in all? _____

The Big City
Circus Is in Town!

Read each problem to see if there is enough information to solve it.

Mark **enough information** or **not enough information**.

Solve the problems that have enough information.

1. There are 40 clowns in the 1:00 circus show and 40 clowns in the 4:00 circus show. There are 8 clowns who perform in both shows. How many clowns are there in all? _____

   enough information   **not enough information**

2. Each animal in the circus has its own cage. The show has 4 elephants and 2 tigers. How many cages will be needed in all if Horseman Joe adds 4 more horses to his Incredible Horse Show? _____

   enough information   **not enough information**

Street Math

Tell if you should **add** or **subtract** to solve each problem.
Then solve the problems.

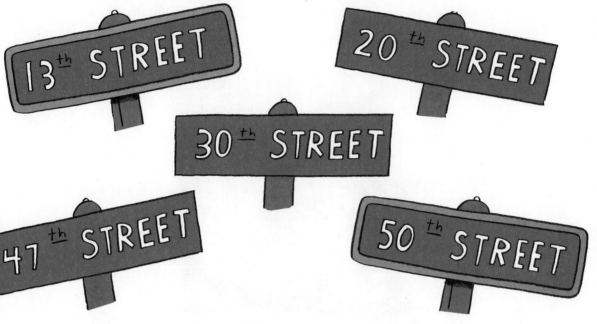

1. Mike has to walk from 13th Street to 20th Street.
   How many blocks does he have to walk? _____

   add   **subtract**

2. Jennifer walked 24 blocks uptown. She started at
   30th Street. What street did she end on? _____

   add   **subtract**

3. Tara will meet a friend at a restaurant on 50th Street.
   How many blocks will Tara have to walk if she starts
   on 47th Street? _____

   add   **subtract**

Sightseeing

Read each problem to see if there is enough information to solve it.
Mark **enough information** or **not enough information**.
Solve the problems that have enough information.

1. The Marcus family went sightseeing for 3 hours today. They saw the Mayor's Palace, the Mega Movie Soundstage, and the City Museum. How much time did they spend at each place? _____

   enough information   **not enough information**

2. After a 2-hour tour of the Mega Movie Soundstage, the Jones family stopped for lunch at the Fame and Fortune Family Restaurant. They waited for 45 minutes to be seated and their lunch took 1 hour. How long did it take from the beginning of the tour to the end of their lunch? _____

   enough information   **not enough information**

Big City Fair

Tell if you should **add** or **subtract** to solve each problem.
Then solve the problems.

There were 4,729 people at the city fair on Saturday.
There were 3,482 people there on Sunday.

1. What was the total number of people at the fair? _____

   add   **subtract**

2. How many more people were at the fair on Saturday
   than on Sunday? _____

   add   **subtract**

3. There were 1,362 people at the fair on Saturday who did not
   go on a ride. How many people enjoyed a ride that
   day? _____

   add   **subtract**

Gotta Get to Class!

Tell if you should **multiply** or **divide** to solve each problem.
Then solve the problems.

Cara takes taxis to and from her art class every Monday, Wednesday, and Friday night. The ride usually costs about $7.50 each way.

1. How much does Cara usually spend
   in one week taking taxis to class? _____

   multiply   **divide**

2. Cara shares a taxi with a friend on the ride home
   from class on Mondays. They split the cost of the
   fare. How much does Cara spend taking a taxi
   home on Mondays? _____

   multiply   **divide**

Movie Action!

The big city is a good place to make movies. Answer the questions.

1. The film crews started working at 6:00 AM. They stopped working at 7:00 PM. How many hours did they work? _____

2. The movie is being shot for 2 full weeks indoors and 4 weeks outdoors. How many days are being filmed indoors?_____

3. If the actors work 8 hours on Monday, 4 hours on Tuesday, and 9 hours on Wednesday, how many hours will they work in all? _____

At the Corner Store

Read and solve each problem.

1. George has $9.50. He buys one toy car and one baseball.
   How much money does he have left? _____

2. Martin has $10.00. He buys one kite and one baseball.
   How much money does he have left? _____

3. How much does it cost to buy two toy cars and one kite? _____

Transportation Troubles

Read and solve each problem. Mark the correct time on the clocks.

1. Martha's bus was supposed to pick her up at 8:05 AM. It was
    10 minutes late. Draw the time on the clock that the bus picked
    Martha up.

2. John got on the bus at 3:45 PM. He got off the bus 1 hour and 20
    minutes later. Draw the time on the clock that John got off the bus.

Bus Riders

The chart shows how many people rode on Mr. Smith's bus last week.
Use the chart to solve the problems.

DAY	NUMBER OF RIDERS
Monday	689
Tuesday	600
Wednesday	527
Thursday	702
Friday	623
Saturday	321
Sunday	305

1. Which day of the week was busiest on Mr. Smith's bus? _____

2. Which days had less than 650 riders but more than 550? _____

3. How many riders rode Mr. Smith's bus during the weekend? _____

4. Which day had closest to 675 riders? _____

Let's Go Shopping!

Tasha has $8.50. Make a list of all the different things she can buy if she uses up all of the money. She can only buy each item once.

_____

_____

_____

Animals at the Park

Read the sentences below. Fill in the chart to show
which animals live in the park in the winter and summer.

ANIMALS IN THE PARK	Summer	winter
Squirrels	X	X
Ducks		
Birds		
Fish		
Geese		

Squirrels live in the park all year.

Ducks do not live in the park during winter.

Birds live in the park all year.

Fish live in the pond in the park all year.

Geese live in the park in the summer only.

Which animals leave the park in winter?

_____

Concert in the Park

Solve the problems.

1. Vera and Hank sit in the 5th row to watch the concert. Joe and
    Betty sit 12 rows behind them. Jesse sits 27 rows behind Hank.
    How many rows apart are Joe and Jesse? _____

2. The guitar player on the stage also sings. Tonight he sings 14
    songs while playing the guitar, and he plays only guitar on 18
    songs. There are only 2 songs that he does not play at all.
    How many songs does the band play tonight? _____

Tiptoe Through the Tulips

The city likes to keep tulips blooming along Main Street. Answer the questions about how many tulips are needed during one season.

There are 139 tulips planted in front of Town Hall. There are 53 tulips planted in the intersection of Main Street and Park Street. There are 80 tulips planted in front of office buildings.

1. The tulips have to be replaced once during the season. How many tulips are needed during one season? _____

2. The gardener bought red tulips for Town Hall, yellow tulips for the intersection, and orange tulips for the office buildings. How many more orange tulips will there be than yellow ones? _____

Sports in the Big City

The big city has the best sports teams anywhere.
Graph how many wins each team has gotten.

The football team is in second place. They have 34 wins.

The baseball team is in first place. They have 41 wins.

The hockey team is in third place. They have 30 wins.

What information are you missing to find out which team had more wins than losses? _____

Fresh Fruit and Veggies

Joe sells fresh fruit and vegetables at the City Farmer's Market. Every week Joe sells onions, squash, apples, pears, and watermelon. This week, Joe sold twice as much of each of the foods than he did last week.

1. If Joe sold 50 squash this week, how many did he sell last week? _____

2. If Joe sold 80 apples last week, how many did he sell this week? _____

3. If Joe sold 40 pears last week and twice as many this week, how many pears did he sell in the last two weeks all together? _____

Autumn in the Park

It takes a team of workers all day to rake the leaves in the park.

Use the table to solve the problems.

WORKERS

		Mike	Tara	Bruce	John	Joey
Square Yards of Leaves	AM	150	148	138	84	141
	PM	75	82	98	158	76

1. Who raked the most square yards of leaves? _____

2. Who raked more in the morning than Tara? _____

3. How many more square yards did Bruce rake than Joey? _____

4. Who raked more than Joey in the afternoon, but less than Bruce? _____

Art Show Today

Adam and Carla went to the City Art Museum. They saw sculptures, paintings, and photographs. Answer the questions about them.

Adam and Carla saw a room filled with 20 paintings, 6 sculptures, and 18 photographs. The room next to it had 3 times as many sculptures.

1. How many sculptures were in the second room? _____

2. How many sculptures were in both rooms together? _____

Library Hours

Read the sign for the library's hours. Answer the questions.

Monday	9 AM to 6 PM
Tuesday	9 AM to 6 PM
Wednesday	9 AM to 6 PM
Thursday	12 PM to 9 PM
Friday	9 AM to 6 PM
Saturday	10 AM to 5 PM
Sunday	closed

1. It takes Jane 15 minutes to walk to the library. On what day will she have to leave at 11:45 to get there when it opens? _____

2. On which days can she not be there at 5:30 PM?

   _____

3. How many fewer hours is the library open on Saturday than on other days? _____

Big City Taxi

Read each problem to see if there is enough information to solve it.
Mark **enough information** or **not enough information**.
Solve the problems that have enough information.

1. The taxi charges $1.40 for the first mile and $.75 for every mile after that. How much would it cost to take a taxi 6 miles? _____

   enough information   **not enough information**

2. The taxi driver picks up 4 people in an hour. Each ride costs less than $10.00. What did each rider pay? _____

   enough information   **not enough information**

3. On Saturday, the taxi driver picked up 20 more people than he had the day before. On Thursday, he picked up 22 people, which is 4 more than he picked up on Friday. How many people did he pick up on Saturday? _____

   enough information   **not enough information**

Big City Bus Route

Read the story below. Put check marks on the chart to show where the bus driver must stop along his route.

PLACES TO STOP	BUS STOPPED
School	
Grocery Store	
Movie Theater	
Library	
Exercise Center	
Clothing Store	
Sports Stadium	

Jeff has to stop at the grocery store. Mrs. Beetle has to stop at the library, but not the school. Ben wants to go to the movie theater, but his mother says they will go to the exercise center instead. The soccer team will stop at the school and the sports stadium. Mimi will not stop at the clothing store, but she has to stop at the grocery store instead.

1. How many stops will the bus make? _____

2. Are there any stops that the bus will not make?
   What are they? _____

Dog Walkers

Sandy is a dog walker for her apartment building. She walks dogs during the day while their owners are at work. The chart shows how often she walks the dogs.

Dog Walking Schedule	9:00	12:00	3:00	6:00
Muffy	X	X	X	
Poogle	X	X	X	X
Max	X			X
Miss Biffy	X		X	
Puff Ball	X	X	X	
Shakespeare	X	X	X	
Yippie	X		X	X

1. Which dogs are walked more than Max, but less than Poogle?

_____

2. How many times a day does Shakespeare see Miss Biffy?_____

Sale Days

Howard's Department Store is having a sale. Cross out the information that is not needed to solve the problems. Then solve the problems.

1. Umbrellas are on sale today for $3.00 off from 9 AM to noon. It is going to rain in the afternoon. How much will an umbrella that is originally $16.00 be at 10 AM? _____

2. Shoes are on sale for half off. Becky buys 3 pairs of shoes that originally cost $40.00 each. She buys 1 pair in 2 colors. How much did she pay for the 3 pairs of shoes? _____

Subway Riddle

Read the paragraph and answer the questions.

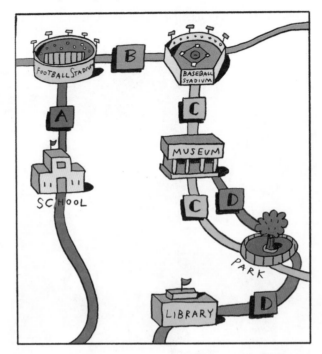

The A train stops at the football stadium and the school. The B train stops at the football stadium and the baseball stadium. The C train stops at the museum, the park, and the baseball stadium. The D train stops at the park, the museum, and the library.

1. What trains could you take to get to the museum?

   _____

2. If you took the B train, where could you go? _____

   _____

3. Which train goes to both the library and the park?

   _____

People Watching

Sam is doing a school project. He is keeping track of how many people pass by one intersection in one hour.

Time	People Passed Once
1st quarter hour	30
2nd quarter hour	38
3rd quarter hour	47
4th quarter hour	80

1. How many people passed by in one hour? _____

2. How many people passed in the first half hour? _____

3. How many people passed in the second half hour? _____

Tours, Tours, Tours!

Read the paragraph and answer the questions.

Susan gives tours of the city's three most popular tourist sites. She gives tours of the City Aquarium, the City Gardens, and City Hall.

1. Susan gave 15 tours in the last week. If she gave the same number of tours at each place, how many tours did she give at the aquarium? _____

2. A tour of the gardens takes 50 minutes. A tour of the aquarium takes 50 minutes. A tour of City Hall takes 30 minutes. Which will take longer? _____
   a) 2 tours of City Hall and a tour of the gardens
   b) a tour of the gardens and the aquarium

Hockey Mania

Read and solve each problem.

There's a big hockey game tonight! The stadium has 1,400 seats.

1. In section A, 120 tickets were sold. In section B, 545 tickets were sold. In section C, 720 tickets were sold. Is the game sold out? _____

2. The stadium has already sold 1,050 tickets for tomorrow night's game. How many tickets are still available? _____

Late Night Fun

The city is open late!

Quickie Burger is open until 11 PM. Ice Cream Heaven is open until 10 PM. Bobbie's Books is open until 9 PM. All of the stores are on the same city block.

1. Judy and Melanie want to go to the bookstore, then have a burger for dinner, and ice cream for dessert. They will spend about an hour at each place. What is the latest time they can get to the bookstore? _____

2. Sani is done eating at Ice Cream Heaven at 8:30 PM. How much time does he have to look for a book at the bookstore? _____

All Mapped Out

Use the map to answer the questions.

1. Estimate how many blocks it is from the
    Farmer's Market to the Opera House. _____

2. Jake is at the Opera House. About how many
    blocks is he from Howard's store? _____

Restaurant in the Park

Use the menu to answer the questions.

☆ MENU ☆

MAIN DISHES

HARRY'S CHICKEN	$ 8.95
ROSIE'S TURKEY	$ 9.95
VEGETABLE DUMPLINGS	$ 7.50
SPINACH RAVIOLI	$ 7.00

SIDE DISHES

MASHED POTATOES	$ 2.50
SALAD	$ 2.00
STRING BEANS	$ 1.50

BEVERAGES

ALL DRINKS	$ 1.50

☆ ☆ ☆

1. How much is a Harry's Chicken, a side salad, and a drink? _____

2. Bob is paying for his brother's meal. They each get a Rosie's Turkey, a side salad, mashed potatoes, and a drink. How much does Bob owe? _____

3. List the meals that Paul can get for exactly $11.00 if he gets a main dish, a side dish, and a drink. _____

_____

Now for Some Dessert!

Mama's Bake Shop has the best desserts in town.
Use the menu to answer the questions.

Menu

Chocolate Pie	$4.^{25}
Apple Crumble Cake	$3.^{75}
Mystery Mousse	$4.^{00}
Strawberry Tart	$3.^{25}
Mama's Cookies	$2.^{50}
Mama's Cookies with milk	$3.^{50}

1. Jeanne and her friends ordered 2 pieces of chocolate pie,
   1 piece of apple crumble cake, and 1 plate of Mama's
   cookies with milk. How much do they owe? _____

2. Tonight the chef replaced the strawberry tart with a peach tart
   for 75¢ more. How much would 3 of them cost? _____

3. How many mystery mousses can you buy with $14.00? _____

Big City Ballet

Sara's class is going to see the ballet.

1. Each school bus holds 60 students. There are 300 students signed up for the trip. How many school buses are needed? _____

2. The show starts at 11:00. The students need to get to the ballet by 10:45. It takes one and a half hours to drive from the school to the theater. When is the latest that the buses can leave the school? _____

Skyscraper, Skyscraper

Compare the height of each building and answer the questions.

The Johnson Building is 45 stories taller than the Benjamin Building. The James Tower is 18 stories taller than the Johnson Building. The Robin Convention Center is 10 stories shorter than the Benjamin Building. The Benjamin Building is 30 stories tall.

1. Write the order of the buildings, from shortest to tallest.

    _____

    _____

2. How many stories tall is the James Tower? _____

3. How many more stories is the James Tower than the Benjamin Building? _____

4. How much shorter is the Robin Convention Center than the Johnson Building? _____

Let's Go Skating

Jessica is having an ice-skating birthday party in the park!

1. It costs $5.00 to rent ice skates at the rink. There are 12 guests at the party, including Jessica. Three of the guests brought their own skates. How much will Jessica's mother pay for all of the children to rent ice skates? _____

2. Jessica's party is 3 hours long. The skating rink has to be cleaned every half hour. How many times will the ice be cleaned while Jessica's party is there? _____

Ride the Subway

Answer the questions.

1. One subway car has 35 seats. All of the seats are filled and there are 15 people standing. How many people are in the subway car? _____

2. It takes 20 minutes for the subway to go from uptown to downtown. How long will it take for the train to make the trip two times? _____

3. There are 35 people in the subway car. At the next stop, 2 people get off and 5 people get on. Now how many people are in the subway car? _____

Early Morning Delivery

Trucks deliver the newspaper early in the morning.

1. There were 30 bundles of newspapers on the truck. The driver left 4 bundles at the first stop and 3 bundles at the second stop. How many bundles of newspapers were left on the truck? _____

2. The truck driver had to make 4 stops on Warner Street and 6 stops on Park Place. How many more stops does he have to make if he makes 35 stops in all? _____

Rooftop Garden

Read the paragraph and answer the questions.

Leslie planted a garden on her rooftop. She planted 4 tomato plants, 3 rows of carrots, and 5 rows of green beans.

1. How many carrots did she plant if there are 6 plants in each row? _____

2. How many more tomato plants will she have to plant if she wants to have 9 in all? _____

3. There are 5 green bean plants in each row. How many green bean plants are there in all? _____

Little Ballerina

Use the chart to solve the problems.

	PRACTICES	SHOW TIMES
Monday	2:00 – 4:00	
Tuesday	3:00 – 6:00	7:30
Wednesday		3:00
Thursday		
Friday	2:00 – 4:00	7:30
Saturday		2:00
Sunday		4:00

Melissa is a ballerina in a big theater show.

Look at her schedule for practices and show times.

1. On which days does Melissa have both a practice and a show?

   _____

2. On which days does she have either a practice or a show?

   _____

3. How many hours a week does Melissa go to practices? _____

Pennant Fever

Read the paragraph and answer the questions.

The city football team is going to be in the playoffs! So many people are expected to go to the game that the stadium wants to double all of their food orders for the big day.

1. How many hot dogs will they have to make if they usually make 2,300 hot dogs? _____

2. How many cups will they need to order if they usually sell 4,250 drinks? _____

3. How many pretzels will they need to make if they usually make 3,270? _____

Pumpkin Festival

Read the paragraph and answer the questions.

Once a year there is a pumpkin festival in the park. This year they have some very big pumpkins. The biggest one is 155 pounds! The next largest pumpkin is 45 pounds lighter. The average size of a pumpkin at the festival is 23 pounds.

1. How many pounds is the second largest pumpkin at the festival?_____

2. How many more pounds is the largest pumpkin than an average-sized pumpkin? _____

3. How many more pounds is the second largest pumpkin than an average-sized pumpkin? _____

Ice Cream Vendor

Read the paragraph and answer the questions.

Mr. Mac owns an ice cream truck in the park. On Tuesday, 130 people bought ice cream from him. On Wednesday, 122 people bought ice cream from him. On Thursday, 105 people bought ice cream from him.

1. How many more people bought ice cream on Tuesday than on Thursday? _____

2. How many people bought ice cream on Wednesday and Thursday? _____

3. On Friday, Mr. Mac sold ice cream to the most people of all. On that day, 185 people bought ice cream from him. How many more people bought on Friday than bought on his slowest day? _____

Let's Race!

Read the paragraph and answer the questions.

1. Theresa's class had running races in the park. She finished the race 3 yards ahead of James. James finished the race 4 yards ahead of Mike. How far ahead of Mike did Theresa finish the race? _____

2. Tonya and Bobbie were part of the relay race. The entire distance of the race was 740 yards. If Bobbie ran 420 yards, how many yards did Tonya run? _____

City Marathon

Use the chart to answer the questions.

Runners	Place Finished	Home State	Number of Times in Race
Monica	23rd	Idaho	4
Ralph	52nd	Florida	7
Enid	3rd	Florida	9
Jasper	15th	Nebraska	10

1. Which marathon runner from Florida ran in more races? _____

2. Which runner ran the fewest number of races? _____

3. What state is the runner who is between 10th and 20th place from? _____

4. How many people finished the race between Ralph and Jasper? _____

Big City Theater

Read the paragraph and answer the questions.

It takes 5,692 tiny lights to light up the Big City Theater sign. Robert replaces the light bulbs when they need to be replaced.

1. In January, Robert replaced 429 bulbs. In February, he replaced 238 bulbs. In March, he replaced 532 bulbs. In which month did Robert replace more than double the number of bulbs that he replaced in February? _____

2. If 1,789 bulbs are used around the outside border of the sign, how many are used in other places? _____

Off to School

Read the paragraph and answer the questions.

Rosa's school is 7 blocks from her home. On her way to school she meets David after 4 blocks. They meet Oscar after another 2 blocks. They all arrive at school together.

1. How many blocks does Oscar walk with his friends to school? _____

2. How many blocks do Rosa and David walk together? _____

3. Does Rosa walk more blocks with David, with Oscar, or by herself?

_____

Visiting an Office

Read the paragraph and answer the questions.

Isabelle visits her mother at work on the 27th floor of an office building. It takes 10 seconds to get from floor to floor.

1. How long does it take to get from the
   1st floor to the 7th floor? _____

2. How long does it take to get from the
   11th floor to the 25th floor? _____

3. How long does it take Isabelle to get from the
   1st floor to her mother's office? _____

Team Pizza

Read the paragraph and answer the questions.

City Pizza is the best pizzeria in town. Julie and her softball team stop there to eat after a game. There are 16 girls on the team. One pizza has 8 slices.

1. If everyone has one slice, how many pizzas should they order for the team? _____

2. Coach, Veronica, and Maggie want 2 slices each. Plus, Coach wants to take a pizza home for his family. How many pizzas should they order? _____

Answer Key

Page 4
1. 6
2. 2
3. 4

Page 5
1. a
2. b

Page 6
1. 39
2. 12
3. 269

Page 7
"The subway stops at the museum, but not the school" is crossed out; 3

Page 8
1. 6
2. 50

SUBWAY STOPS
8th Street
18th Street
28th Street
38th Street
48th Street
58th Street
68th Street
78th Street
88th Street
98th Street
108th Street

Page 9
1. not enough information
2. 6; enough information
3. not enough information

Page 10
1. $6.00
2. $8.00
3. $8.00

Page 11
1. 6; enough information
2. not enough information
3. 6 miles; enough information

Page 12
1. 3
2. No, because they're both at the same time.
3. No, because the planets show ends at 2:45.

Page 13
1. 1; a
2. 35; c

Page 14
1. "Nachos are $1.50" is crossed out; $1.50
2. "It is the fifth inning" is crossed out; 5

Page 15
1. 20
2. 125
3. 214

Page 16
1. 72; enough information
2. 10; enough information

Page 17
1. 7; subtract

2. 54th; add
3. 3; subtract

Page 18
1. not enough information
2. 3 hours and 45 minutes; enough information

Page 19
1. 8,211; add
2. 1,247; subtract
3. 3,367; subtract

Page 20
1. $45.00; multiply
2. $3.75; divide

Page 21
1. 13
2. 14
3. 21

Page 22
1. $4.25
2. $1.75
3. $8.25

Page 23
1.

2.

Page 24
1. Thursday
2. Tuesday and Friday

3. 626
4. Monday

Page 25
book, soda, card, popcorn, newspaper

book, sandwich, card

book, sandwich, newspaper

Page 26

ducks, geese

Page 27
1. 15
2. 34

Page 28
1. 544
2. 27

Page 29

The total number of games played, or the number of losses.

Page 30
1. 25
2. 160
3. 120

Page 31
1. John
2. Mike
3. 19
4. Tara

Page 32
1. 18
2. 24

Page 33
1. Thursday
2. Saturday and Sunday
3. 2

Page 34
1. $5.15; enough information
2. not enough information
3. 38; enough information

Page 35

PLACES TO STOP	BUS STOPPED
School	√
Grocery Store	√
Movie Theater	
Library	√
Exercise Center	√
Clothing Store	
Sports Stadium	√

1. 5
2. Yes. The movie theater and the clothing store.

Page 36
1. Muffy, Puff Ball, Shakespeare, Yippie
2. 2

Page 37
1. "It is going to rain in the afternoon" is crossed out; $13.00
2. "She buys 1 pair in 2 colors" is crossed out; $60.00

Page 38
1. C or D trains
2. football stadium or baseball stadium
3. D train

Page 39
1. 195
2. 68
3. 127

Page 40
1. 5
2. a

Page 41
1. no
2. 350

Page 42
1. 7PM
2. a half hour

Page 43
1. 20 blocks
2. 10 blocks

Page 44
1. $12.45
2. $31.90
3. vegetable dumplings, salad, drink

   spinach ravioli, mashed potatoes, drink

Page 45
1. $15.75
2. $12.00
3. 3

Page 46
1. 5
2. 9:15

Page 47
1. Robin Convention Center, Benjamin Building, Johnson Building, James Tower
2. 93
3. 63
4. 55

Page 48
1. $45.00
2. 6 times

Page 49
1. 50
2. 40 minutes
3. 38

Page 50
1. 23
2. 25

Page 51
1. 18
2. 5
3. 25

Page 52
1. Tuesday and Friday
2. Monday, Wednesday, Saturday, Sunday
3. 7

Page 53
1. 4,600
2. 8,500
3. 6,540

Page 54
1. 110
2. 132
3. 87

Page 55
1. 25
2. 227
3. 80

Page 56
1. 7 yards
2. 320

Page 57
1. Enid
2. Monica
3. Nebraska
4. 37

Page 58
1. March
2. 3,903

Page 59
1. 1
2. 3
3. by herself

Page 60
1. 60 seconds or 1 minute
2. 140 seconds or 2 minutes and 20 seconds
3. 260 seconds or 4 minutes and 20 seconds

Page 61
1. 2
2. 4

Congratulations,

_____!
(Name)

You're an excellent problem solver!